D0884196

AMAZING TRAINS

Subway Trains

by Christina Leighton

Note to Librarians, Teachers, and Parents:

Blastoff! Readers are carefully developed by literacy experts and combine standards-based content with developmentally appropriate text.

Level 1 provides the most support through repetition of high-frequency words, light text, predictable sentence patterns, and strong visual support.

Level 2 offers early readers a bit more challenge through varied simple sentences, increased text load, and less repetition of high-frequency words.

Level 3 advances early-fluent readers toward fluency through increased text and concept load, less reliance on visuals, longer sentences, and more literary language.

Level 4 builds reading stamina by providing more text per page, increased use of punctuation, greater variation in sentence patterns, and increasingly challenging vocabulary.

Level 5 encourages children to move from "learning to read" to "reading to learn" by providing even more text, varied writing styles, and less familiar topics.

Whichever book is right for your reader, Blastoff! Readers are the perfect books to build confidence and encourage a love of reading that will last a lifetime!

This edition first published in 2018 by Bellwether Media, Inc.

No part of this publication may be reproduced in whole or in part without written permission of the publisher. For information regarding permission, write to Bellwether Media, Inc., Attention: Permissions Department, 5357 Penn Avenue South, Minneapolis, MN 55419.

Library of Congress Cataloging-in-Publication Data

LC record for Subway Trains available at https://lccn.loc.gov/2016052937

Text copyright © 2018 by Bellwether Media, Inc. BLASTOFF! READERS and associated logos are trademarks and/or registered trademarks of Bellwether Media, Inc. SCHOLASTIC, CHILDREN'S PRESS, and associated logos are trademarks and/or registered trademarks of Scholastic Inc.

Editor: Nathan Sommer   Designer: Lois Stanfield

Printed in the United States of America, North Mankato, MN.

Table of Contents

WHAT ARE SUBWAY TRAINS?

Subway trains work mostly underground. They are often hidden below busy city streets!

subway train
underground

Subway trains usually take short trips. They carry riders from **station** to station.

Main Stree
Flushing

4

Boarding Area

subway station

BUILT FOR TUNNELS

These trains travel through deep **tunnels**. Their lights shine through the dark.

tunnel

Subway wheels follow tracks. The tracks help connect the city!

DEEPEST SUBWAY STATION IN NEW YORK

151 feet (46 meters)

Statue of Liberty

180 feet (55 meters)

191st Street Subway Station

tracks

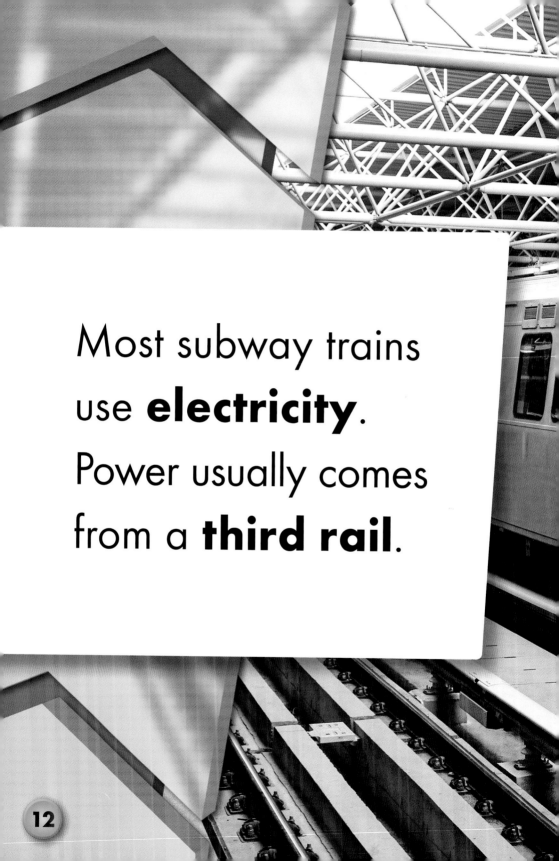

Most subway trains use **electricity**. Power usually comes from a **third rail**.

third rail

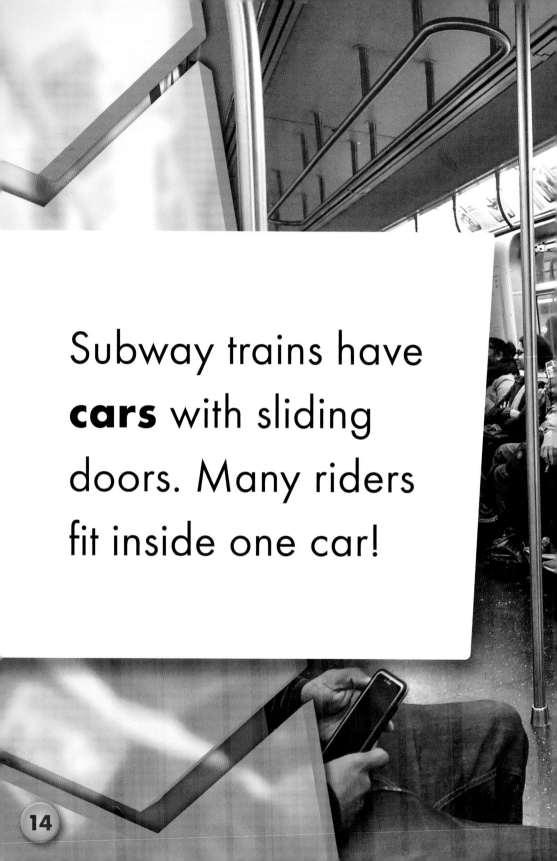

Subway trains have **cars** with sliding doors. Many riders fit inside one car!

subway car

The trains let people on and off at station **platforms**.

station platform

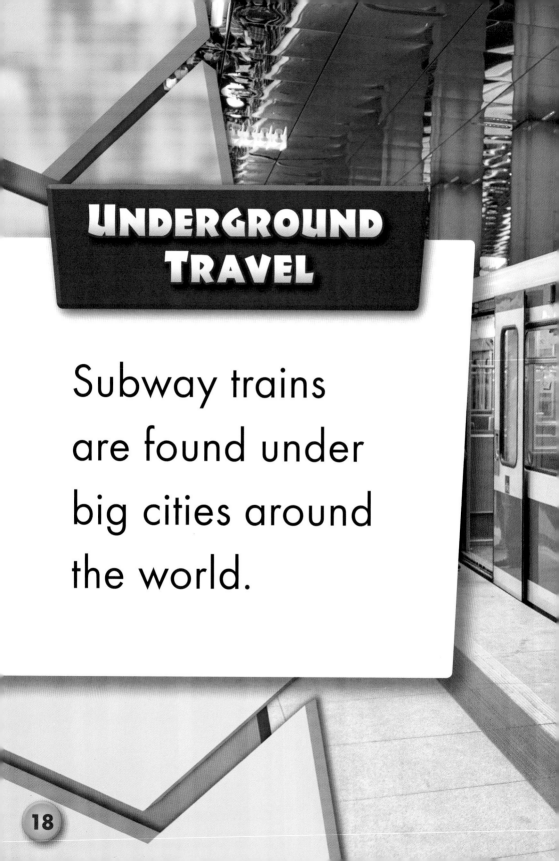

UNDERGROUND TRAVEL

Subway trains are found under big cities around the world.

subway in Munich, Germany

Every day, millions of people count on subways for travel!

Glossary

cars

vehicles pulled by a train

station

a place where people get on and off a train

electricity

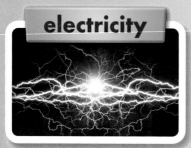

a form of energy that gives power

third rail

an extra bar on train tracks that gives power to trains

platforms

flat areas where people stand and wait for subway trains

tunnels

paths underground that subways travel through

To Learn More

AT THE LIBRARY

Clapper, Nikki Bruno. *City Trains*. North Mankato, Minn.: Capstone Press, 2016.

Lassieur, Allison. *Subways in Action*. Mankato, Minn.: Capstone Press, 2012.

Peters, Elisa. *Let's Ride the Subway!* New York, N.Y.: PowerKids Press, 2015.

ON THE WEB

Learning more about subway trains is as easy as 1, 2, 3.

1. Go to www.factsurfer.com.

2. Enter "subway trains" into the search box.

3. Click the "Surf" button and you will see a list of related web sites.

With factsurfer.com, finding more information is just a click away.

Index